ADDRESS

ON

THE CULTURE DEMANDED BY THE AGE.

BY

FREDERIC DE PEYSTER, LL.D.

DELIVERED BEFORE

The Alumni Association of Columbia College.

New York:
PRINTED BY JOHN F. TROW.
1869.

THE CULTURE DEMANDED BY THE AGE.

BROTHERS OF THE ALUMNI ASSOCIATION
OF COLUMBIA COLLEGE:—

THERE are few associations so delightful as those which cluster around the venerable mother, from whom our intellectual life is, in so important a sense, derived. These associations carry us back to the freshness and vigor of our youth. They recall the time when life presented itself in anticipation, only as a series of brilliant victories; and when a golden glow suffused the morning sky of our early years. The remembrance of generous friendships, some of them only strengthened by the lapse of time, and others sundered only by the separations of death, touches our hearts, even now, with a strange delight. Nor can we forget, under the influence of these associations, the peculiar charm, which at that time attended the acquisition of certain departments of knowledge. It is indeed the common impression that most young men, in college, are averse to intellectual effort, and acquire knowledge only under the pressure of the severest discipline. This is not the case. There are few who do not have a keen relish for those studies which, under wise instruction, open themselves naturally to the mind. Especially is this the case with those studies which address themselves in any sense to the imagination. There is scarcely any enjoyment in life comparable to the refined and elevating pleasure, which accompanies these early exercises of the mental powers. All the freshness of this peculiar happiness these associations are powerful to recall; and though each period of life, even on to the extremest age, has its own privileges and its own mission in the adorning and perfecting of character, yet this period, when we were nurtured by this august mother of us all, must, in our recollection of it, ever thrill and animate our hearts. We realize in the happy retrospect the fulfilment of the prophecy, so familiar in our college days—

"Hæc olim meminisse juvabit."

Of this our venerable *Alma Mater* we may well be proud, and rejoice that we are permitted to number ourselves among her sons. For more than a century she has been the prolific and faithful parent of a progeny of large-hearted and large-minded men. We cannot examine our family record as her *Alumni*, without feeling what a privilege it is to be numbered as brethren with so many of those she is proud to call her sons. I cannot speak of the living, though the thought of them is vivid in my mind. I rejoice in the young men whom she has reared; and who, under the influence of her wise culture, are prepared to discharge the mission to which educated men are called in this wonderful age. I rejoice in the honorable record of so many of her sons now advanced in life, and whose power of beneficent influence only increases with the diminution of bodily strength. Venerable in years, in learning, and in usefulness, they command the homage of our grateful admiration and love.

It would be impossible to speak, on this occasion, in fitting terms, of the long list of the departed *Alumni* or officers of this our *Alma Mater*. Some recent names there are, that we cannot but recall to mind. The varied acquirements and culture of Renwick, the classic erudition and strongly-marked manliness of Anthon, the liberal and courtly character and bearing of King, and the wide culture and critical taste of McVickar, will ever be remembered in connection with this Institution. The memory of the noble Anthon is embalmed in the biography, happily as ably executed by his worthy successor in the Jay Professorship. May some hand, as skilful, present us with a similar memorial of our late Emeritus professor—McVickar, over whose mortal remains we recently witnessed the last solemn services of the Church, in which he had faithfully ministered for more than a half-century!

Passing back in memory to the youthful days of our now venerable mother, among the distinguished sons whom she then gave to the world, were two of such conspicuous greatness and imperishable national renown, that their names alone would give immortality to any Institution with which they were connected. For how many of the most important principles which have entered into our political organization are we not indebted to Alexander Hamilton! For how much of the spirit of liberty and sympathy with freemen, freedom and progress, are we not indebted to John

Jay! In the struggles which accompanied the establishment of our republican institutions, these sons of Columbia were indeed

"Geminos, duo fulmina belli."

Coming down from the early history of our College to more modern times, another conspicuous Alumnus, prominent among the eminent statesmen of our country, is *De Witt Clinton.* With his national reputation is associated the remembrance of the substantial blessings which his genius, influence, and efforts conferred upon his native State by the system of internal improvements, inaugurated and perfected by him. He has indelibly stamped his name on that successful enterprise which has materially aided in making the City of New York the chief mart of the nation, by intermingling our inland seas with the oceans that encircle the globe; and thereby it has become a more influential link in the stupendous chain which embraces within its fold the commerce of the world.

But to pass from these allusions which, though only of family interest, as it were, are pardonable when the sons of our common mother meet together, it seems to me that the subject which would most naturally suggest itself to the mind, and which it is perhaps the most important to consider on such an occasion, is

THE CULTURE DEMANDED BY OUR AGE.

It may be necessary perhaps at the outset to vindicate the idea that our age could possibly require a different culture from those which have preceded it.

That such an idea should present itself at such a time is not to be wondered at. It would be the greatest marvel if it were otherwise. For this is a period in which there is a universal questioning of what has heretofore challenged the belief of mankind. Every form of opinion and of practice is now required to justify its existence. It would be strange indeed if a subject, so fraught with importance to human welfare as culture or education, should escape the ordeal to which everything else is subjected.

But it is not merely inevitable that the prevailing methods of culture should be challenged in this critical age. There are also facts which render it reasonable to suppose that the vastly different conditions of life, in modern times, should make a new system of culture, better adapted to these changed conditions, desirable if not absolutely necessary. The relations of man to nature are entirely different from what they have ever been. These relations are both speculative and practical. The knowledge of nature has been amazingly augmented within a comparatively short period of time. Numerous discoveries, of the most wonderful character, of the principles and laws which govern the universe, have been made; and investigations are now vigorously pushed in regions never thought of a century ago. A man cannot be a truly educated man without knowing something of these new fields and processes of inquiry. But no man can gain even a superficial acquaintance with them, without departing widely from the traditional system of education.

Besides this it is a fact which will hardly be disputed, that the prevailing system grew out of no philosophy of nature and of man; and that the philosophical arguments which are oftentimes urged in their behalf, were an after-thought, and not the considerations out of which grew the method of culture, which has so long maintained its hold on the world. The question, therefore, has very great force, at the present day, whether the large results which we have reached in philosophy should not be made the basis upon which our system of culture should be reared.

These considerations, among many others, have led to a violent assault in our day upon the predominance of the classics and mathematics in our prevalent system of education; and to an exaltation, in comparison, of the various departments of scientific study. The controversy is now going on, more fiercely perhaps than ever. It has already largely modified the present systems. These modifications are likely to be still further increased in the future.

One great difficulty is, that the controversy is generally carried on as if the truth lay wholly upon the one side or the other. Too often the advocates of one view, claim that the only object of culture is mental discipline; while the advocates of the other claim as tenaciously that it is the acquisition of useful knowledge. Accordingly it is asserted on the one side, that the only means of culture, of any great account, is the study of the Mathematics and Classics, and on the other that it is the study of Nature. But more than this, it is claimed on each side that, even if the view of the other, as to the object of culture, should be correct, its own method would be, even then, to be preferred. It is a repetition in principle of the old story of the suspended shield, brass on one side and iron on the other; which one knight, riding in one direction, maintained to be wholly brass; and another riding in an opposite direction, to be wholly iron; and at last, when they had nearly killed each other in their furious strife, each found that both were equally wrong, and both were equally right.

For it is pre-eminently true, in this controversy, that truth is to be found in both the systems, which are here in antagonistic relations. In a single word, it is the object of education both to discipline the mind and to impart useful knowledge; and the true method of education is the study, not only of the Mathematics and Classics, but of Nature also.

It is evident, however, that there is to be a re-adjustment of the relations between these different objects of study and investigation, and that very important changes are certain to be introduced into our educational systems. These facts render it exceedingly important that the whole subject should be carefully considered, by those who are the friends of truly liberal culture

The first thing to be determined is what is the true object of culture or education. This I should, and I think without contradiction, define to be the progress of man in his normal destiny, and in the direction of his highest perfection and happiness.

The proper method of inquiry on this subject is evidently to start with the facts of which we are in possession in reference to the nature of man; and then determine what culture is best adapted to bring him into harmony with the sphere in which he is placed.

The philosophy of *man* should be the basis of the philosophy of *education.*

Man is, then, to be considered under three aspects physical, intellectual and moral.

It is of course impossible to draw distinct and definite lines between these different departments of the complex nature of man. The physical passes by imperceptible gradations into the intellectual, and the intellectual into the moral. At the same time there is a general distinction so manifest as to render separate consideration possible and necessary.

I. THE PHYSICAL NATURE OF MAN.

The fact that man has a physical organization is too vastly important a one to be overlooked, or treated superficially in a system of education. The normal destiny of man, which we have seen to be the object of culture, demands a state of physical health and vigor. And yet what a commentary is it upon the prevalent system of education, that an educated man is supposed to be almost necessarily a man of irritable nerves and precarious health. If the prevalent system tends to the diminution of physical vigor, it is enough to condemn it, and in the most emphatic manner; just so far as such is its result. It is a principle which cannot reasonably be questioned that a true system of education should promote, as far as possible, the physical well being of man. To question this is to assume that one part of our nature cannot be cultivated except at the expense of another. And this indeed is just what is assumed in the prevalent ideas on the subject. It is commonly supposed that mental application is unfavorable to physical health, and that physical vigor is most likely to be attained by a life devoted to physical exercises. To persons holding these views, the savage, who is almost without mental development, is the ideal of physical manhood. It is time that such notions were abandoned; and that the respect too often paid to ill health as indicative of mental culture should be treated as a superstition.

It is true that excessive application of the mind is liable to injure the body, and so is excessive eating. But would any one think of urging that eating, within due bounds, is unfavorable to bodily health? So far is the due exercise of the mental powers from being detrimental to our physical welfare, it is one of the prime conditions upon which that welfare is secured. The results of most thorough investigation show that the progress of education and consequent civilization have been accompanied by an increase in the size, the vigor and the longevity of men.

The general principle is that the true culture of one department of man's nature cannot be at the expense of another; but that the culture of these different departments is mutually beneficial. Under this general principle, it appears that physical culture as *an end* is promoted by mental culture as *a means.*

But, besides this, physical culture must be promoted as a means to mental culture as an end. The mind works at an immense disadvantage unless the physical organism is sound. Perhaps there may be, for a time, intenser mental activity in connection with abnormal or diseased states of the nervous system; and

2

so the mind works with tremendous energy in the delirium of brain-fever; but in either case it is like the excessive working of an engine, from which the regulating power is gone, and which can end only in ruin. To *sustain* power of this kind is impossible. Permanent power to eliminate strong, manly, symmetrical thought, requires a sound physical organization.

There is exquisite beauty oftentimes in the autumn leaf; but it is the product of disease, soon to be followed by decay and death.

A very common misconception is that an organization which is sensitive to external impressions, while it is favorable to an intellectual and especially a poetical temperament, is necessarily less sound and capable of endurance than one which is more gross in its structure. This depends altogether upon the *cause* by which the sensitiveness is occasioned. If it is the consequence of a morbid condition of the nervous system, it is symptomatic of disease, and not of health; but on the other hand it is also true that the most highly and perfectly organized natures are the most impressible; for in them there is necessarily the most of the spiritual element, or the vital principle. The most delicate and refined organism claims for itself therefore the most of health, endurance and vigor.

The intimate and inextricable relations between mind and body show the necessity of wise physical culture, in order to the highest mental efficiency. The operations of the mind record themselves, as it were, in lines grooved in the very substance of the brain. Uncounted millions of these lines intersect each other, and the *power* of retaining and reproducing processes of thought, depends upon the permanence of these lines, which in its turn depends upon the character and condition of the substance of the brain. Now, there is no part of the wonderful organism of man which is more affected by those agencies which have relation to health, than the brain. The food we eat, the air we breathe, the exercise we take, the business we transact, the pleasures we enjoy, all modify the condition of that organ of the mind, and thus affect directly the permanence and tenacity of mental impressions.

These various considerations show the vast importance, in a system of comprehensive culture, of physical training. It is amazing to think of the undeveloped capacities for improvement which exist in reference to every thing which relates to health, and of the possible accession of mental power, when the various conditions upon which our physical well-being is dependent, are thoroughly understood.

One suggestion of a practical character may not be out of place, relating as it does to a danger to which sedentary men are peculiarly exposed. It seems to be now established that the value of mere muscular training, in and for itself, has been greatly over-estimated; and that such training in the case of scholars especially, is apt to be attended with disastrous results. Prize-fighters do not enjoy better health than the average of men; probably do not live as long. There is a great principle involved here, which may apply also to mental culture; that exercise or training, whether of the body or the mind, should not be proposed as an end, but should be secured in connection with sports or useful work. The swinging of dumbbells, or protracted walks, or rowing for mere muscular development, are far inferior, as means of a true physical culture, to athletic sports involving genuine play, or even hard work for some directly practical end.

A false view of Christianity under the influence of which the body has been treated, first with contempt, and then with depreciation, and from the effects of which society has not yet recovered, has interfered most seriously with physical culture. But now the true view of the sacredness of the body, the view taught explicitly in the New Testament, is beginning again to be understood. The discoveries in modern science have given new emphasis to the declaration of the Psalmist: "Behold, I am fearfully and wonderfully made." This marvellous organism, so related to the material on the one hand, and the spiritual on the other that it is a true *microcosm*, is the visible, tangible thing, in which the soul dwells and through which it is revealed. In the renewed man, it is the temple of the Holy Ghost. We are to abide in this temple, to see that no defilement desecrates it, that passion does not mar it, nor evil indulgence shatter it till it crumbles into the dust: and we are reverently to guard and adorn it, and to make it pure and beautiful for the Divinity, who condescends to make it His home, in which He delights to dwell.

II.—INTELLECTUAL CULTURE.

I pass from the consideration of the body as the organ of the mind, to that of the mind itself. The principles of education which apply to mental culture are necessarily more numerous and complex than those which apply to the culture of our physical organization. The subject, therefore, here enlarges itself, like a narrow stream which flows on into the broader circumference of the lake.

The first point which demands our attention is the method by which the powers and faculties of the mind may best be strengthened. We cannot divide the mind itself into different faculties, even in idea. These faculties of which we speak are simply the mind working in a certain way. In the consideration of these faculties and powers we naturally consider those first which are first developed. These come under the general head of Powers of Observation.

These powers are exercised when the mind consciously acts upon the impressions received through the senses. The exercise of them presupposes an inquiring attitude of mind, and the fixing of itself upon some object presented for its investigation. It is amazing what a difference comes to exist in these powers by simple cultivation. Uneducated people, or those who are not accustomed to notice carefully the objects by which they are surrounded, will give, in perfect sincerity, the most varied and even contradictory accounts of the same thing. Miss Nightingale furnishes an illustration of this in her admirable work on the office of a Nurse, when she says that very few persons have their powers of observation sufficiently cultivated to be able to give an accurate account of the symptoms of a sick person.

There can be no doubt but that there might be an immense gain of mental efficiency by the systematic culture of these powers in the young. It is too often supposed that the first step in education is to turn the thoughts *within*, and to lead the mind to occupy itself with ideas. On the contrary, the first step in education is observation, the fixing of the mind intensely upon external objects. The mind of the child is to be put in relation with nature, which furnishes at once the library which he is first to study. The power of observation is of course strengthened by the habit of observing. The attention of the child, therefore, instead of being directed primarily to books, should be directed and fixed upon natural objects. Take almost any object in nature, a tree, or a stone, or a flower, or an animal, and lead a child to notice it carefully—to tell its shape, its size as compared with some other object, its color or colors, and any thing which may be especially characteristic of it, and you furnish an exercise which is at once delightful and salutary to the mind. For those children who are so unfortunate in this respect as to live in the city, this culture nevertheless is not altogether hopeless. Houses, although there is a sad want of variety in them, may be taken as objects of observation, and a lamp or telegraph post even, if the attention is fixed long and earnestly upon it until it is thoroughly observed, may be made a most important aid in this culture.

Professor Agassiz is in the habit, it is said, of keeping the most promising of his pupils for six months in intense observation of the bones of the turtle. This study is highly pleasurable as well as beneficial, for the simple reason that it is permitting and encouraging the mind to a development of itself in a natural direction.

The immense advantage of such habits of observation is that it enables a mind thus trained, to grasp at a glance all the peculiar characteristics of an object; nay, the same habit passes over into the region of thought, and an idea, in all its relations, is almost *intuitively* comprehended.

It would not be easy to exaggerate the importance of this culture as a foundation for all mental discipline. It is evident, also, that in this respect there is a most lamentable need to be supplied. We constantly find men of the largest mental capacities, who are incompetent to grasp the few practical details of a subject, for want of this early training. Men of thought, of reflection and of learning, have oftentimes grown up with scarcely any knowledge of the most common objects by which we are surrounded. They are, therefore, as helpless as infants in regard to any matter with which these objects are connected. The worst of it is that this ignorance is very commonly regarded as an indication of culture, so that a man who knows nothing about a horse and is perfectly incapable of the least control over him, is thought to be a learned man, if he has mastered all that ancient poets, in unknown languages, have told us of the winged horse *Pegasus*. It is impossible that there can ever be a true idea of education so long as such a sentiment is entertained. Just so far as introspection and retrospection are made to take the place of observation, just so far will man be untrue to that process of culture which God has provided for him. For God has not placed us in the midst of this marvellous system of material objects without a purpose, willing that we should be indifferent to them.

There is not an insect, or a leaf, or a pebble, or a grain of sand, or a bird, or a wave breaking on the sea-shore, upon which He has not lovingly bestowed His infinite care and skill. He has filled the vastness of space with His innumerable worlds; holding them and moving them in our very sight, and glorifying them with an indescribable splendor, that we may observe and study that which He has created; for in studying these we learn more and more of the Divine Creator.

But in addition to these powers of observation, there are powers of *reflection* to be cultivated. The observation of facts is absolutely essential, and the ability to observe them is indispensable, but it is only the foundation of the mental processes, which should follow. Something must be done with these facts. Under the influence of mere observation they lie in the mind disconnected and isolated. There is no perception of the mental relations of these facts. But inasmuch as all phenomena are linked together by laws, and all constitute one harmonious system, these laws become the proper subject of investigation as the next step in the process of mental culture. This requires the exercise of the powers of reflection. The conditions under which these powers must be exercised are furnished in the mind itself. The mind necessarily apprehends all objects under certain relations. They are conceived as related to time and space. The mind works upon these by certain fixed and definite methods. It cannot work otherwise. The processes employed must be those of comparison, analysis, and synthesis. Memory and imagination must be exercised; and all this is necessary to the attainment of definite mental results. The question, therefore, is how the mind may best become habituated to these processes. It should be remembered here that these processes do not necessarily involve the *discovery* of the laws of phenomena, but they do require the comprehension of laws already discovered. It is in this direction that they are employed in the vast majority of cases.

In the consideration of this question, it is evident that there must be some classification of phenomena arranged in the order of their comparative simplicity or complexity. For it is a law of the mind that it passes most readily from the simple to the complex. Without attempting, then, any thing like a complete classification of the phenomena presented to the mind, there is an order in which facts may be arranged, which is founded in the nature of things.

We have then a series of facts which arrange themselves naturally in some such order as that of the Inorganic and Organic; the organic including the whole range of animal life, culminating in man and society. Moral phenomena are not here taken into account, for their peculiar relation to this series will presently be considered.

It is evident that there is here an order of progressive complexity. The simple phenomena with which we begin, soon become exceedingly complicated. But it is also evident that the mind advances easily along this path, because there is a preadaptation to this method in its very nature. Now here we find the order in which facts are to be observed and reflected upon, with a view to the best cultivation of the Powers of Observation and Reflection, and the attainment of the most satisfactory results. Travelling along this line, we shall find *all* that has been made the subject of human study; but each department brought by this natural law of arrangement into its proper place, and standing in its own comparative importance.

The classification of phenomena to which reference has been made suggests an analogy, which doubtless exists between the order of creation and the true order of mental development and culture. *Creation* proceeded from the simple to the complex. There is first the inorganic and then the organic, in its constantly increasing complexity. The order of mental development corresponds to this. If this correspondence is successively followed, the exercise of the powers of observation and reflection upon the lowest forms of inorganic existence, and then upon each higher step in the widening series, is easy, pleasurable, and attended with the most gratifying results.

Beside this, there is a physiological fact which has already been described, which shows the immense importance of continuity in culture; so that each stage of the progress may grow out of that which preceded it. Since the process of thought changes the very substance of the brain, and repetitions of the same thought tend to fasten it more firmly in the memory, the desirableness is evident of carrying on our mental processes in the direction of lines of previous thought, already marked out in the brain. It is the demand of a physiological as well as a mental law, that there should be a continuous series of development, each growing logically out of the one preceding it, and the whole series corresponding to the order of creation in the natural world.

These principles introduce us to what it seems to me is the truly philosophical order in which the mind is to occupy itself with different departments of study. Supposing these principles to be correct, let us see how they can be practically applied in the case of one whom we wish to lead through the various stages of a truly liberal education.

The first department of study then to which the attention of a child, who has learned the meaning of ordinary words, should be directed, is that of *inorganic* nature. Of course this study is to be carried on in the simplest possible way, and is not to dispense with a more thorough study of the same branches in after years. The point is, that here are the subjects with which study should *commence;* and that certain elementary ideas should be formed of them, as the first step in mental culture. The true method then would be to familiarize the child, in the first place, with the prominent facts in astronomy, in mineralogy and geology, and in *inorganic* chemistry. The idea of a *child* engaged in the study of these sciences may perhaps provoke a smile; but why not as properly as that he should be studying Grammar or Arithmetic or Languages! Will any one undertake to say that these facts and relations of the visible, tangible world are not as readily comprehended by a child, as the more abstruse facts and relations of Language and Numbers? After the rare success of that noble son of science, the late Michael Faraday, in expressing some of the highest facts of science in language universally comprehensible, it is idle to doubt the power of any child of ordinary ability to understand statements, which will convey a knowledge of the elementary principles and facts of these sciences. The great point however which is here gained, is that children enjoy these studies. Who ever saw an intelligent child, who, though he might yawn all day, without learning any thing, over an Arithmetic or a Grammar, would not instantly brighten up and be all attention, if some object in nature is to be examined, or the operation of some skillful machinery to be explained?

But this will suffice to indicate the nature of those studies which come first in the order of mental culture. The next step in the series is easy and natural. It takes us from the inorganic to the organic World. The process is uninterrupted and continuous; for in nature the transition is not arbitrary and abrupt. The *inorganic* passes up into the *organic* by imperceptible gradations. So the mind moves along this pathway which in nature is provided for it, and ascends to the comprehension of higher and more complicated facts.

This stage of the development of mental culture introduces us to such sciences as Botany, and Geology so far as it relates to fossil remains, and to Physiology as related to the lower animals; for the science of Man constitutes a stage by itself. In these, if taken in their natural order, there is the same fascination as in the *inorganic* sciences; or rather, the charm increases with the greater variety, beauty, and complexity of the facts.

It becomes necessary even in the *child's* study of inorganic nature to introduce the study of numbers, as necessary to express the relations of facts to each other. This study should be pursued in this higher stage, just so far as it is necessary for that purpose, and not primarily for mental discipline. It is exceedingly doubtful whether it is a suitable discipline for the reasoning powers; for it has to do only with demonstrative evidence, while man everywhere else is obliged to use his reasoning powers upon *moral* evidence, or the balancing of probabilities. But as furnishing a key by which to unlock the secrets of nature, and as a means of marvellous concentration of processes of thought into brief and simple expressions, it is of immeasurable importance and value. It is also most important to remember that in this connection, and when used for such a purpose, even the higher mathematics, instead of being repulsive as they often are to so many minds, become invested with an almost poetic charm, which appeals, as figures and quantities are not usually supposed to do, to the loftiest exercise of the imagination.

Having thus alluded to the relations of mathematics to this development of mental culture, we ascend to a still higher stage in the department of the sciences of organic nature. We come to the consideration of *man*, the noblest work of God in the sphere of things which is cognizable by us. The pupil whom we are leading in imagination through a system of universal culture, comes from the study of physiology among the lower orders of animal life to the study of physiology in man. He passes naturally and therefore with delight from one to the other; and as physiology, as applied to man, presents itself, he sees the vast interest and importance of the new problems to which he is introduced. But, as it is my purpose merely to suggest the outline of a method of philosophical culture, it is not necessary that we should linger here upon the phenomena, vastly interesting though they are, of *Physiology*, as applied to man; we can pass on at once to *Psychology*, as the next department which demands our attention. There is no abrupt transition here, but following the path which nature points out, we are led naturally and easily, by the mere development of processes already familiar to us, from the higher facts of physiology to the lower manifestations of psychological phenomena.

It is at this point, and it is an inexpressibly important one in our systems of education, that the study of language naturally and logically comes in. Here it is that certain phenomena, partly physiological and partly psychological, present themselves. Language is preëminently the mediating element between the two. It is to be regarded physiologically as expressed through the organs of speech and as modified by physical condition, and psychologically as the expression of thought and feeling. A vast field is here opened before us, and some general knowledge at least of it must be attained by him who would be a universal student. What we wish to ascertain at this stage of culture is the law under which the *mind* expresses itself. It is the method by which we first become aware of the existence of mind, that here demands our consideration. The first fact which challenges our attention is this, that there are different languages among different races and nations of men. Upon examining these different languages, however, we find that some have a vastly higher claim upon our study than others.

The principle upon which this comparative importance of languages is settled, is a very simple one. Those languages which reveal to us most richly the operations of thought and feeling, or the great motive powers in history, are the languages which have the strongest claim upon our attention. The claims in these respects of the three great languages of antiquity, the Hebrew, the Greek, and the Latin, cannot reasonably be questioned. In the Hebrew we are admitted to the thought of a people isolated from other nations, passing through a marvellous history and under the influence of an extraordinary degree of *supernatural* ideas. In the Greek we find how a people thought and felt, whose dominant principle was a love for the beautiful; and in whom the metaphysical tendency reached its highest point. In the Latin, we read the thought of a vast imperial nation, with which action is the prevailing idea, and which rules the destiny of the world. I am now speaking, let it be remembered, not of the literature of these different nations, but simply of the language of each as a medium for the expression of thought. It is the study of mental phenomena which is involved in the study which we are now considering; and through the investigation of these phenomena we arrive at some of the laws which govern the mind.

As we have now indicated the place of the study of the mathematics and the ancient languages in a system of universal culture, it may be well to say a few words more as to the principles by which that relative position is determined. This is the more important as the whole controversy, as to the place of the mathematics and classics, in a system of universal culture, hinges upon this point.

The proper subject, then, of all study is phenomena, as they are presented to us, in this divinely created system in which we are placed. The order in which these phenomena are to be investigated is determined by their relative simplicity or complexity, and is indicated, as we have seen, in the very process of creation. The Divine Being has himself laid out the plan of culture for man in the works which He has created. If this is so, then the pursuit of any study, out of its place in the prescribed order, is in violation of a system established in the very nature of things, and cannot be justified by any supposed advantages it possesses for the discipline of the mind. The mind is best disciplined by a strict adherence to the natural method of culture. The study of mathematics is not directly a study of phenomena, but it is a study of that which is necessary to a comprehension of phenomena, and it becomes more and more complex in the exact ratio of the complexity of the phenomena investigated. This simple principle at once establishes its proper place and relation.

The study of the classics is somewhat different from that of the mathematics in this respect, that it is a study directly of phenomena themselves. The history of the world presents to us certain remarkable facts, among which are the languages of the Hebrew, the Greek, and the Roman. When we come in the progress of our culture to the study of man and of psychology as one of the departments of that study, it is impossible to reach completely satisfactory results without an inquiry as to the modes of thought and feeling which are presented to us in these languages of the ancient world. The value of the study of them is found not merely in the fact that it is an important mental discipline, for that is true of all study which is conformed to the system of culture indicated in nature, but in the fact that it reveals the complex nature of man in some of the most interesting and instructive aspects in which it has ever been presented. In these three languages we find not only indications of a common origin, but we find also the foundations, as it were, of all the languages of the civilized world. It is not easy, therefore, to exaggerate the importance of the study in the relation in which it has now been presented. This importance is of course greatly heightened when we consider the subject of these ancient languages in their social and æsthetical relations. But we are now considering it simply as it comes before us as one step in the system of universal culture, and as the study of some of the most important psychological phenomena which can be presented to the mind.

These suggestions I cannot but regard as important in their bearing upon the question of the relative value of the study of the mathematics and classics as compared with each other, and with other departments of study. But as the mathematics and classics pass on into higher departments of thought, I will reserve what I have to say on that point until the consideration of the whole range of culture is complete.

The next step in the natural gradation of the sciences is Sociology, or the science of society. We pass from the *individual* man to the *community* of man.

No person at all familiar with the present aspect of civilization can fail to appreciate the immense importance to human welfare of this whole class of investigations. New phenomena of the most complex character are, in these modern times, presented in this widely extended field of thought, and new problems consequently demand solution. The minds of men are gradually undergoing a change as to the nature of society, and especially the state or government in which society has its principal expression. And this change is the result of a more careful observance and investigation of social phenomena. It is preëminently necessary that this observance and investigation should be prosecuted far beyond its present limits. In this prosecution we find ourselves in the presence of facts of the greatest complexity as well as of incalculable importance. Take the single science of *Political Economy*, for instance, and the difficulty at present of analyzing and systematizing the vast extent of the phenomena with which it is concerned, is almost incalculable. This difficulty of grasping social phenomena arises more from the want of this system of culture, graduated by the order of succession in natural facts, than from any other cause. The whole range of culture as it has now been presented, is necessary in order to the best preparation for the solution of social problems.

I have intimated that the study of the classics and mathematics is to be continued in connection with the study of society. The complexity of the phenomena to be investigated requires the highest calculus which the mathematics can furnish, and the order of social facts can be understood only from the history of society, to which the classics perhaps contribute the most important element.

Thus far the laws of the development of culture through the study of sciences, which follow each other in a certain order, has been considered. We have found that when this order is conformed to the successive stages of creation in the natural world, it is an organic development, each step in the progress being dependent upon the one preceding. This is the method indicated to us by God in nature, and like all the Divine methods secures the utmost economy of *means* with the largest possible *results.*

But so far the process presents itself as one of mere thought and intellectual inquiry. If a system of culture is to be truly universal, it must embrace the whole nature of man, and address itself not only to the bare intellect, but to the emotions also. It must aim at the appreciation of beauty as well as the discovery of truth. Such a process as we have indicated of mere intellectual without æsthetical culture is like a giant oak without its foliage. The trunk and branches have been developed *organically* from the acorn. All is symmetrical, and indicative of mighty strength; but it is destitute of beauty. When, however, under the genial influences of Spring, the hidden life is evolved, and takes to itself the form of myriads of leaves, glistening in the sunlight, and covering the whole tree with its vast canopy of shade, then it is *beautiful* as well as *strong.* So the *intellectual* needs to be adorned by the results of *æsthetical* culture, and the massive trunk and wide-spreading branches of the sciences to be clothed with leaves of poetry and art.

This form of culture is to be carried on *pari passu* with the scientific culture which we have considered. In fact, it is but supplementary to that. Each stage in the *scientific*, furnishes material and stimulus for *æsthetical* culture. The love and appreciation of the beautiful are to be fostered from the earliest dawn of consciousness; and as this is chiefly accomplished through the culture of the imagination, so we find that the imagination is healthfully excited by the very study of the various sciences following in their natural order. It is only necessary that the mind should be systematically directed to the quality of beauty as well as of truth in nature. The study of the mathematics contributes, when rightly used, as few would believe possible, to the culture of the imagination. For it enables us to grasp and express relations of such vast magnitude as almost to overwhelm the mind, and to arrange them in systems which in their perfection of accuracy impress the mind with a profound sense of the beautiful. It brings the imagination, more nearly than any other process of thought, into the presence of the Infinite.

The study of classical literature contributes powerfully to *æsthetical* culture. This is particularly true of the literature of the Greeks, in which, perhaps more than in any other, the culture of the beautiful has been the predominant idea. No one, especially with the training which the previous culture here indicated would afford, can imbue his mind with that wonderful development of poetry and art of which Homer and Sophocles and Phidias are among the chief exponents, and of which so many works and monuments remain to the present time, without securing a more delicate and refined, as well as a broader sense and appreciation of beauty.

This seems to be the fitting place, before a few closing words in regard to moral culture, to offer a suggestion as to an adjustment of what have been too often regarded as the rival claims of some of these different departments of study.

The plan here indicated, it must be remembered, is one of universal culture; the true method to be used by one who wishes to attain the highest improvement of his faculties, and the largest amount of knowledge. There is a certain ground to be gone over. The order is continuous and progressive, but there are different stages in it which are distinctly defined. It is all the study of phenomena or of that by which phenomena *can* be studied or enjoyed. It would seem as if there must be some principle by which it should be determined, that, while general attention is given to the whole series, to what portions *particular* attention should be devoted. I think such a principle is to be found in the fact that certain studies are more immediately related to human welfare than others. It seems to be reasonable, then, that they should receive a larger proportion than others of our time and thought. There may be indeed a question as to what constitutes human welfare,—whether it is mere material well-being, or intellectual and moral attainment. It includes both. The mathematics and classics contribute to both, but the mathematics best contribute to both when they are studied, not as an end, but as a *means* to the unlocking of the manifold secrets of nature; and the classics also, when a far less amount of thought, than now, is devoted to mere grammatical structure, and more to the ancient languages as expressions of mental phenomena, and to the literatures which they enshrine. But the demands of the present age seem especially to require a thorough investigation of the principles of Physiology and Political Economy. The reason of this will be manifest to a careful observer of the present wants of Society; but without dwelling on this point, let me say that the view which has been taken clearly designates the place of each study in a system of culture, and the order in which they should follow. According to this view, the mathematics are to be pursued from the simpler to the more complex forms, just so fast as the more complex are needed for the investigation of phenomena. In reference to the classics, this view assigns them a more advanced position. Their place is at that point in the progress of culture where Psychology is reached, and they reappear in the science of Society, and also in the higher stages of aesthetical culture.

This process of culture, which widened out like a stream that flows into a wide-spreading lake, as we passed from physical to mental development, narrows again like the stream through which the waters of the lake discharge themselves, as we pass from *mental* to *moral* culture and development. The importance of moral culture, in regard to which I can say but a single word, is found in the fact that *man* is the only moral or religious being on this earth. Plato says that man is an Intelligence served by organs. De Bonald says, coming somewhat nearer the truth, that he is an Intelligence *making use* of organs. A still higher and truer view is that of Pascal, that it is the *morale* which is characteristic of man, and furnishes us with his definition.

Moral culture is not a process of discovery of *truth*, but of conformity to a known and recognized law of *conduct*. It consists in the cultivation of a clear discriminating moral sense, and the formation of habits of moral obedience. Many truths which are the objects of discovery assist and further this culture; but the fundamental principles upon which it is based are original and inherent. The motives to its prosecution are furnished, and the Divine help which is required is revealed in the *Word of God*. It is to commence with our earliest consciousness, to proceed with ever-increasing power in all our subsequent career, and through the beneficent provisions of the Christian religion will prepare us for the destiny of an everlasting life.

Brothers of the Alumni:—I have ventured upon these imperfect suggestions in regard to that which constitutes a complete system of culture, influenced not only by the importance of the subject itself, but also by the conspicuous position which this College occupies in relation to it. Both these considerations impose, it seems to me, a large responsibility upon us. For it lies with us, in a great measure, to enable our *Alma Mater* to exercise her influence *wisely* and *beneficently* for the best good of society. This Institution is situated in the commercial metropolis of this country. It should be so generously endowed and so enlarged in all its appliances, that it may make this city the scientific and literary metropolis also. We are living in a time of rapid changes, when the welfare of society demands the modification of many existing institutions. Undoubtedly many important changes will take place in the system of culture which has been accepted here. We shall do wisely to welcome these changes as the advancing intelligence of our age shall demand them. They will bring larger privileges to those who come after us, than we ourselves have enjoyed. Let us be thankful for that. The community of scholars should be no place for the indulgence of selfish sentiment. We rejoice in the coming light, though our eyes here may not be permitted to behold it.

> "Let knowledge grow from more to more,
> But more of *reverence* in us dwell;
> That *mind* and *soul*, according well,
> May make one music, as before,
>
> "But vaster. * * * *"

Nov. 9, 1868.

www.ingramcontent.com/pod-product-compliance
Lightning Source LLC
LaVergne TN
LVHW011124110826
845150LV00008B/2243